This Wedding Planner Belongs To:

♥   ♥

_____

Initial Planning Phase

IDEAS FOR THEME -a wedding

IDEAS FOR VENUE
Slide ranch

IDEAS FOR COLORS

IDEAS FOR MUSIC

IDEAS FOR RECEPTION

OTHER IDEAS

Notes & Ideas

Wedding Budget Planner

Expense MANAGER

CATEGORY/ITEMS	BUDGET	ACTUAL COST	BALANCE

Wedding Budget Checklist

CATEGORY	BUDGET	ACTUAL COST	DEPOSIT	BALANCE

Wedding Contact List

IMPORTANT VENDOR CONTACTS				
	NAME	**PHONE #**	**EMAIL**	**ADDRESS**
OFFICIANT				
RECEPTION VENUE				
BRIDAL SHOP				
SEAMSTRESS				
FLORIST				
CATERER				
DJ/ENTERTAINMENT				
WEDDING VENUE				
TRANSPORTATION				
OTHER:				
OTHER:				
OTHER:				

NOTES & More

SPECIAL REMINDERS

Planning Snapshot

CEREMONY EXPENSE TRACKER

	BUDGET	COST	DEPOSIT	BALANCE	DUE DATE
OFFICIANT GRATUITY					
MARRIAGE LICENSE					
VENUE COST					
FLOWERS					
DECORATIONS					
OTHER					

NOTES & Reminders

NOTES & REMINDERS

RECEPTION EXPENSE TRACKER

	BUDGET	COST	DEPOSIT	BALANCE	DUE DATE
VENUE FEE					
CATERING/FOOD					
BAR/BEVERAGES					
CAKE/CUTTING FEE					
DECORATIONS					
RENTALS/EXTRAS					
BARTENDER/STAFF					

NOTES & More

SPECIAL REMINDERS

Planning Snapshot

PAPER PRODUCTS EXPENSE TRACKER

	BUDGET	COST	DEPOSIT	BALANCE	DUE DATE
INVITATIONS/CARDS					
POSTAGE COSTS					
THANK YOU CARDS					
PLACE CARDS					
GUESTBOOK					
OTHER					

NOTES *& Reminders*

NOTES & REMINDERS

ENTERTAINMENT EXPENSE TRACKER

	BUDGET	COST	DEPOSIT	BALANCE	DUE DATE
BAND/DJ					
SOUND SYSTEM RENTAL					
VENUE/DANCE RENTAL					
GRATUITIES					
OTHER:					
OTHER:					
OTHER:					

NOTES *& More*

SPECIAL REMINDERS

Planning Snapshot

WEDDING PARTY ATTIRE EXPENSE TRACKER

	BUDGET	COST	DEPOSIT	BALANCE	DUE DATE
WEDDING DRESS					
TUX RENTALS					
BRIDESMAID DRESSES					
SHOES/HEELS					
VEIL/GARTER/OTHER					
ALTERATION COSTS					

NOTES & Reminders

NOTES & REMINDERS

TRANSPORTATION EXPENSE TRACKER

	BUDGET	COST	DEPOSIT	BALANCE	DUE DATE
LIMO RENTAL					
VALET PARKING					
VENUE TRANSPORTATION					
AIRPORT TRANSPORTATION					
OTHER:					
OTHER:					
OTHER:					

NOTES & More

SPECIAL REMINDERS

Planning Snapshot

FLORIST EXPENSE TRACKER					
	BUDGET	COST	DEPOSIT	BALANCE	DUE DATE
BOUQUETS					
VENUE DECORATIONS					
BOUTONNIERES					
VASES/EXTRAS					
TABLE DECORATIONS					
OTHER:					

NOTES & Reminders

NOTES & REMINDERS

OTHER EXPENSE TRACKER					
	BUDGET	COST	DEPOSIT	BALANCE	DUE DATE
PHOTOGRAPHER					
VIDEOGRAPHER					
CATERER					
HAIR/MAKEUP/SALON					
WEDDING RINGS					
WEDDING PARTY GIFTS					
OTHER:					

NOTES & More

SPECIAL REMINDERS

Bride's Planner

HAIR APPOINTMENT

SALON NAME	DATE	TIME	BOOKED FOR:		ADDRESS:
				☐	
				☐	
				☐	

NOTES	

MAKE UP APPOINTMENT

SALON NAME	DATE	TIME	BOOKED FOR:		ADDRESS:
				☐	
				☐	
				☐	

NOTES	

MANICURE/PEDICURE APPOINTMENT

SALON NAME	DATE	TIME	BOOKED FOR:		ADDRESS:
				☐	
				☐	
				☐	

NOTES	

Groom's Planner

HAIR APPOINTMENT

SALON NAME	DATE	TIME	BOOKED FOR:		ADDRESS:
				☐	
				☐	
				☐	

NOTES	

TUX FITTING APPOINTMENT

BUSINESS NAME	DATE	TIME	BOOKED FOR:		ADDRESS:
				☐	
				☐	

NOTES	

OTHER:

BUSINESS NAME	DATE	TIME	BOOKED FOR:		ADDRESS:
				☐	
				☐	
				☐	

NOTES	

Important Dates

DATE:	DATE:	DATE:	REMINDERS
DATE:	**DATE:**	**DATE:**	
DATE:	**DATE:**	**DATE:**	
			NOTES
DATE:	**DATE:**	**DATE:**	
DATE:	**DATE:**	**DATE:**	

Weekly Wedding Planning

WEEK OF: _____

MONDAY

TUESDAY

WEDNESDAY

THURSDAY

FRIDAY

SATURDAY

WEDDING TO DO LIST

- [ ] _____
- [ ] _____
- [ ] _____
- [ ] _____
- [ ] _____
- [ ] _____
- [ ] _____
- [ ] _____
- [ ] _____
- [ ] _____
- [ ] _____
- [ ] _____
- [ ] _____
- [ ] _____
- [ ] _____
- [ ] _____

APPOINTMENTS & MEETINGS

DATE	TIME	VENDOR	PURPOSE

Weekly Wedding Planning

WEEK OF: _____

MONDAY

TUESDAY

WEDNESDAY

THURSDAY

FRIDAY

SATURDAY

WEDDING TO DO LIST

- ☐ _____
- ☐ _____
- ☐ _____
- ☐ _____
- ☐ _____
- ☐ _____
- ☐ _____
- ☐ _____
- ☐ _____
- ☐ _____
- ☐ _____
- ☐ _____
- ☐ _____
- ☐ _____
- ☐ _____
- ☐ _____
- ☐ _____

APPOINTMENTS & MEETINGS

DATE	TIME	VENDOR	PURPOSE

Weekly Wedding Planning

WEEK OF: _____

MONDAY

TUESDAY

WEDNESDAY

THURSDAY

FRIDAY

SATURDAY

WEDDING TO DO LIST

- [ ] _____
- [ ] _____
- [ ] _____
- [ ] _____
- [ ] _____
- [ ] _____
- [ ] _____
- [ ] _____
- [ ] _____
- [ ] _____
- [ ] _____
- [ ] _____
- [ ] _____
- [ ] _____
- [ ] _____

APPOINTMENTS & MEETINGS

DATE	TIME	VENDOR	PURPOSE

Weekly Wedding Planning

WEEK OF: _____

MONDAY

TUESDAY

WEDNESDAY

THURSDAY

FRIDAY

SATURDAY

WEDDING TO DO LIST

- [ ] _____
- [ ] _____
- [ ] _____
- [ ] _____
- [ ] _____
- [ ] _____
- [ ] _____
- [ ] _____
- [ ] _____
- [ ] _____
- [ ] _____
- [ ] _____
- [ ] _____
- [ ] _____
- [ ] _____
- [ ] _____

APPOINTMENTS & MEETINGS

DATE	TIME	VENDOR	PURPOSE

Weekly Wedding Planning

WEEK OF: _____

MONDAY

WEDDING TO DO LIST

- [ ] _____
- [ ] _____
- [ ] _____
- [ ] _____
- [ ] _____
- [ ] _____
- [ ] _____
- [ ] _____
- [ ] _____
- [ ] _____
- [ ] _____
- [ ] _____
- [ ] _____
- [ ] _____
- [ ] _____

TUESDAY

WEDNESDAY

THURSDAY

APPOINTMENTS & MEETINGS

DATE	TIME	VENDOR	PURPOSE

FRIDAY

SATURDAY

Weekly Wedding Planning

WEEK OF: _____

MONDAY

TUESDAY

WEDNESDAY

THURSDAY

FRIDAY

SATURDAY

WEDDING TO DO LIST

- [ ]
- [ ]
- [ ]
- [ ]
- [ ]
- [ ]
- [ ]
- [ ]
- [ ]
- [ ]
- [ ]
- [ ]
- [ ]
- [ ]
- [ ]

APPOINTMENTS & MEETINGS

DATE	TIME	VENDOR	PURPOSE

Weekly Wedding Planning

WEEK OF: _____

MONDAY

TUESDAY

WEDNESDAY

THURSDAY

FRIDAY

SATURDAY

WEDDING TO DO LIST

- [ ] _____
- [ ] _____
- [ ] _____
- [ ] _____
- [ ] _____
- [ ] _____
- [ ] _____
- [ ] _____
- [ ] _____
- [ ] _____
- [ ] _____
- [ ] _____
- [ ] _____
- [ ] _____
- [ ] _____
- [ ] _____

APPOINTMENTS & MEETINGS

DATE	TIME	VENDOR	PURPOSE

Weekly Wedding Planning

WEEK OF: _____

MONDAY

TUESDAY

WEDNESDAY

THURSDAY

FRIDAY

SATURDAY

WEDDING TO DO LIST

- ☐ _____
- ☐ _____
- ☐ _____
- ☐ _____
- ☐ _____
- ☐ _____
- ☐ _____
- ☐ _____
- ☐ _____
- ☐ _____
- ☐ _____
- ☐ _____
- ☐ _____
- ☐ _____
- ☐ _____

APPOINTMENTS & MEETINGS

DATE	TIME	VENDOR	PURPOSE

Weekly Wedding Planning

WEEK OF: _____

MONDAY

TUESDAY

WEDNESDAY

THURSDAY

FRIDAY

SATURDAY

WEDDING TO DO LIST

☐ _____
☐ _____
☐ _____
☐ _____
☐ _____
☐ _____
☐ _____
☐ _____
☐ _____
☐ _____
☐ _____
☐ _____
☐ _____
☐ _____
☐ _____

APPOINTMENTS & MEETINGS

DATE	TIME	VENDOR	PURPOSE

Weekly Wedding Planning

WEEK OF: _____

MONDAY

TUESDAY

WEDNESDAY

THURSDAY

FRIDAY

SATURDAY

WEDDING TO DO LIST

- [ ] _____
- [ ] _____
- [ ] _____
- [ ] _____
- [ ] _____
- [ ] _____
- [ ] _____
- [ ] _____
- [ ] _____
- [ ] _____
- [ ] _____
- [ ] _____
- [ ] _____
- [ ] _____
- [ ] _____

APPOINTMENTS & MEETINGS

DATE	TIME	VENDOR	PURPOSE

Weekly Wedding Planning

WEEK OF: _____

MONDAY

TUESDAY

WEDNESDAY

THURSDAY

FRIDAY

SATURDAY

WEDDING TO DO LIST

☐ _____
☐ _____
☐ _____
☐ _____
☐ _____
☐ _____
☐ _____
☐ _____
☐ _____
☐ _____
☐ _____
☐ _____
☐ _____
☐ _____
☐ _____
☐ _____

APPOINTMENTS & MEETINGS

DATE	TIME	VENDOR	PURPOSE

Weekly Wedding Planning

WEEK OF: _____

MONDAY

TUESDAY

WEDNESDAY

THURSDAY

FRIDAY

SATURDAY

WEDDING TO DO LIST

- [ ] _____
- [ ] _____
- [ ] _____
- [ ] _____
- [ ] _____
- [ ] _____
- [ ] _____
- [ ] _____
- [ ] _____
- [ ] _____
- [ ] _____
- [ ] _____
- [ ] _____
- [ ] _____

APPOINTMENTS & MEETINGS

DATE	TIME	VENDOR	PURPOSE

Weekly Wedding Planning

WEEK OF: _____

MONDAY

WEDDING TO DO LIST

- [ ] _____
- [ ] _____
- [ ] _____
- [ ] _____
- [ ] _____
- [ ] _____
- [ ] _____
- [ ] _____
- [ ] _____
- [ ] _____
- [ ] _____
- [ ] _____
- [ ] _____
- [ ] _____
- [ ] _____
- [ ] _____

TUESDAY

WEDNESDAY

THURSDAY

APPOINTMENTS & MEETINGS			
DATE	TIME	VENDOR	PURPOSE

FRIDAY

SATURDAY

Weekly Wedding Planning

WEEK OF: _____

MONDAY

TUESDAY

WEDNESDAY

THURSDAY

FRIDAY

SATURDAY

WEDDING TO DO LIST

- [ ] _____
- [ ] _____
- [ ] _____
- [ ] _____
- [ ] _____
- [ ] _____
- [ ] _____
- [ ] _____
- [ ] _____
- [ ] _____
- [ ] _____
- [ ] _____
- [ ] _____
- [ ] _____
- [ ] _____
- [ ] _____

APPOINTMENTS & MEETINGS

DATE	TIME	VENDOR	PURPOSE

Weekly Wedding Planning

WEEK OF: _____

MONDAY

TUESDAY

WEDNESDAY

THURSDAY

FRIDAY

SATURDAY

WEDDING TO DO LIST

- ☐ _____
- ☐ _____
- ☐ _____
- ☐ _____
- ☐ _____
- ☐ _____
- ☐ _____
- ☐ _____
- ☐ _____
- ☐ _____
- ☐ _____
- ☐ _____
- ☐ _____
- ☐ _____
- ☐ _____
- ☐ _____

APPOINTMENTS & MEETINGS

DATE	TIME	VENDOR	PURPOSE

Weekly Wedding Planning

WEEK OF: ....

MONDAY

WEDDING TO DO LIST

- [ ] ....
- [ ] ....
- [ ] ....
- [ ] ....
- [ ] ....
- [ ] ....
- [ ] ....
- [ ] ....
- [ ] ....
- [ ] ....
- [ ] ....
- [ ] ....
- [ ] ....
- [ ] ....
- [ ] ....

TUESDAY

WEDNESDAY

THURSDAY

APPOINTMENTS & MEETINGS			
DATE	TIME	VENDOR	PURPOSE

FRIDAY

SATURDAY

Weekly Wedding Planning

WEEK OF: _____

MONDAY

WEDDING TO DO LIST

- [ ] _____
- [ ] _____
- [ ] _____
- [ ] _____
- [ ] _____
- [ ] _____
- [ ] _____
- [ ] _____
- [ ] _____
- [ ] _____
- [ ] _____
- [ ] _____
- [ ] _____
- [ ] _____
- [ ] _____

TUESDAY

WEDNESDAY

THURSDAY

FRIDAY

SATURDAY

APPOINTMENTS & MEETINGS

DATE	TIME	VENDOR	PURPOSE

Weekly Wedding Planning

WEEK OF: _____

MONDAY

TUESDAY

WEDNESDAY

THURSDAY

FRIDAY

SATURDAY

WEDDING TO DO LIST

☐ _____
☐ _____
☐ _____
☐ _____
☐ _____
☐ _____
☐ _____
☐ _____
☐ _____
☐ _____
☐ _____
☐ _____
☐ _____
☐ _____
☐ _____
☐ _____

APPOINTMENTS & MEETINGS

DATE	TIME	VENDOR	PURPOSE

Weekly Wedding Planning

WEEK OF: _____

MONDAY

TUESDAY

WEDNESDAY

THURSDAY

FRIDAY

SATURDAY

WEDDING TO DO LIST

- [ ] _____
- [ ] _____
- [ ] _____
- [ ] _____
- [ ] _____
- [ ] _____
- [ ] _____
- [ ] _____
- [ ] _____
- [ ] _____
- [ ] _____
- [ ] _____
- [ ] _____
- [ ] _____
- [ ] _____

APPOINTMENTS & MEETINGS

DATE	TIME	VENDOR	PURPOSE

Weekly Wedding Planning

WEEK OF: _____

MONDAY

TUESDAY

WEDNESDAY

THURSDAY

FRIDAY

SATURDAY

WEDDING TO DO LIST

- [ ] _____
- [ ] _____
- [ ] _____
- [ ] _____
- [ ] _____
- [ ] _____
- [ ] _____
- [ ] _____
- [ ] _____
- [ ] _____
- [ ] _____
- [ ] _____
- [ ] _____
- [ ] _____
- [ ] _____
- [ ] _____

APPOINTMENTS & MEETINGS

DATE	TIME	VENDOR	PURPOSE

Wedding Planner

- PLANNING GUIDELINE -

12 Months BEFORE WEDDING

☐ SET THE DATE	☐ CONSIDER FLORISTS	☐ CONSIDER MUSIC CHOICES
☐ SET YOUR BUDGET	☐ RESEARCH CATERERS	☐ DECIDE ON OFFICIANT
☐ CONSIDER WEDDING THEMES	☐ DECIDE ON OFFICIANT	☐ CONSIDER TRANSPORTATION
☐ PLAN ENGAGEMENT PARTY	☐ CREATE INITIAL GUEST LIST	☐ CREATE INITIAL GUEST LIST
☐ RESEARCH POSSIBLE VENUES	☐ ~~CHOOSE WEDDING PARTY~~	☐ ~~CHOOSE WEDDING PARTY~~
☐ START RESEARCHING GOWNS	☐ CONSIDER ACCESSORIES	☐ ~~BRIDEMAIDS GOWNS~~
☐ RESEARCH PHOTOGRAPHERS	☐ REGISTER WITH GIFT REGISTRY	☐ BOOK TENTATIVE HOTELS
☐ RESEARCH VIDEOGRAPHERS	☐ DISCUSS HONEYMOON IDEAS	☐ CONSIDER BEAUTY SALONS
☐ RESEARCH DJS/ENTERTAINMENT	☐ RESEARCH WEDDING RINGS	☐ CONSIDER SHOES & OTHER

Things To Do	Status

TOP PRIORITIES

NOTES & IDEAS

APPOINTMENTS & REMINDERS

Wedding Planner

- PLANNING GUIDELINE -

- [ ] FINALIZE GUEST LIST
- [ ] ORDER INVITATIONS
- [ ] PLAN YOUR RECEPTION
- [ ] BOOK PHOTOGRAPHER
- [ ] BOOK VIDEOGRAPHER
- [ ] CHOOSE WEDDING GOWN

- [ ] ORDER BRIDESMAIDS DRESSES
- [ ] RESERVE TUXEDOS
- [ ] ARRANGE TRANSPORTATION
- [ ] BOOK WEDDING VENUE
- [ ] BOOK RECEPTION VENUE
- [ ] PLAN HONEYMOON

- [ ] BOOK FLORIST
- [ ] BOOK DJ/ENTERTAINMENT
- [ ] BOOK CATERER
- [ ] CHOOSE WEDDING CAKE
- [ ] BOOK OFFICIANT
- [ ] BOOK ROOMS FOR GUESTS

Things To Do	Status

TOP PRIORITIES

NOTES & IDEAS

APPOINTMENTS & REMINDERS

Wedding Planner

6 *Months* BEFORE WEDDING

- PLANNING GUIDELINE -

- [ ] ORDER THANK YOU NOTES
- [ ] REVIEW RECEPTION DETAILS
- [ ] MAKE APPT FOR FITTING
- [ ] CONFIRM BRIDAL DRESSES
- [ ] OBTAIN MARRIAGE LICENSE
- [ ] BOOK HAIR STYLIST

- [ ] BOOK NAIL SALON
- [ ] CONFIRM MUSIC SELECTION
- [ ] WRITE VOWS
- [ ] PLAN BRIDAL SHOWER
- [ ] PLAN REHEARSAL
- [ ] BOOK REHEARSAL DINNER

- [ ] SHOP FOR WEDDING RINGS
- [ ] PLAN DECORATIONS
- [ ] CHOOSE BOUQUET TYPE
- [ ] FINALIZE GUEST LIST
- [ ] UPDATE PASSPORTS
- [ ] CONFIRM HOTEL ROOMS

Things To Do	Status

TOP PRIORITIES

NOTES & IDEAS

APPOINTMENTS & REMINDERS

Wedding Planner

4 Months BEFORE WEDDING

- PLANNING GUIDELINE -

- [ ] MAIL OUT INVITATIONS
- [ ] MEET WITH OFFICIANT
- [ ] BUY WEDDING FAVORS
- [ ] BUY WEDDING PARTY GIFTS
- [ ] PURCHASE SHOES
- [ ] FINALIZE THANK YOU CARDS

- [ ] FINALIZE HONEYMOON PLANS
- [ ] ATTEND FIRST DRESS FITTING
- [ ] FINALIZE VOWS
- [ ] FINALIZE RECEPTION MENU
- [ ] KEEP TRACK OF RSVPS
- [ ] BOOK PHOTO SESSION

- [ ] CONFIRM CATERER
- [ ] FINALIZE RING FITTING
- [ ] CONFIRM FLOWERS
- [ ] CONFIRM BAND
- [ ] SHOP FOR HONEYMOON
- [ ] BUY GARTER BELT

Things To Do	Status

TOP PRIORITIES

NOTES & IDEAS

APPOINTMENTS & REMINDERS

Wedding Planner

- PLANNING GUIDELINE -

- [ ] CHOOSE YOUR MC
- [ ] REQUEST SPECIAL TOASTS
- [ ] ARRANGE TRANSPORTATION
- [ ] CHOOSE YOUR HAIR STYLE
- [ ] CHOOSE YOUR NAIL COLOR
- [ ] ATTEND BRIDAL SHOWER

- [ ] CONFIRM CAKE CHOICES
- [ ] CONFIRM MENU (FINAL)
- [ ] CONFIRM SEATING
- [ ] CONFIRM VIDEOGRAPHER
- [ ] ARRANGE LEGAL DOCS
- [ ] FINALIZE WEDDING DUTIES

- [ ] CONFIRM BRIDESMAID DRESSES
- [ ] MEET WITH DJ/MC
- [ ] FINAL DRESS FITTING
- [ ] WRAP WEDDIING PARTY GIFTS
- [ ] CONFIRM FINAL GUEST COUNT
- [ ] CREATE WEDDING SCHEDULE

Things To Do	Status

TOP PRIORITIES

NOTES & IDEAS

APPOINTMENTS & REMINDERS

Wedding Planner

- PLANNING GUIDELINE -

- [ ] PAYMENT TO VENDORS
- [ ] PACK FOR HONEYMOON
- [ ] CONFIRM HOTEL RESERVATION
- [ ] GIVE SCHEDULE TO PARTY
- [ ] DELIVER LICENSE TO OFFICIANT
- [ ] CONFIRM WITH VENDORS

- [ ] PICK UP WEDDING DRESS
- [ ] PICK UP TUXEDOS
- [ ] GIVE MUSIC LIST TO DJ/BAND
- [ ] CONFIRM SHOES/HEELS FIT
- [ ] CONFIRM TRANSPORTATION
- [ ] MONEY FOR GRATUITIES

- [ ] COMPLETE MAKE UP TRIAL
- [ ] CONFIRM RINGS FIT
- [ ] CONFIRM TRAVEL PLANS
- [ ] CONFIRM HOTELS FOR GUESTS
- [ ] OTHER: _____
- [ ] OTHER: _____

Things To Do	Status

TOP PRIORITIES

NOTES & IDEAS

APPOINTMENTS & REMINDERS

Wedding Planner

- PLANNING GUIDELINE -

1 Day BEFORE WEDDING

- [ ] ATTEND REHEARSAL DINNER
- [ ] FINISH HONEYMOON PACKING
- [ ] GREET OUT OF TOWN GUESTS

- [ ] GET MANICURE/PEDICURE
- [ ] CHECK ON WEDDING VENUE
- [ ] CHECK WEATHER TO PREPARE

- [ ] GIVE GIFTS TO WEDDING PARTY
- [ ] CONFIRM RINGS FIT
- [ ] GET A GOOD NIGHT'S SLEEP

Things To Do	Status

TOP PRIORITIES

NOTES & IDEAS

APPOINTMENTS & REMINDERS

Your Special Day!

Day of WEDDING

- [ ] GET YOUR HAIR DONE
- [ ] GET YOUR MAKE UP DONE

- [ ] HAVE A LIGHT BREAKFAST
- [ ] MEET WITH BRIDAL PARTY

- [ ] GIVE RINGS TO BEST MAN
- [ ] ENJOY YOUR SPECIAL DAY!

MR ❤ MRS

Wedding Attire Planner

WEDDING ATTIRE EXPENSE TRACKER

ITEM/PURCHASE	STATUS ✓	DATE PAID	TOTAL COST

NOTES & REMINDERS

TOTAL COST:

Notes:

WEDDING ATTIRE DETAILS

Venue Planner

VENUE EXPENSE TRACKER

ITEM/PURCHASE	STATUS ✓	DATE PAID	TOTAL COST

NOTES & REMINDERS	
	TOTAL COST:

Notes:

Mr & Mrs

VENUE PLANNING DETAILS

Catering Planner

CATERING EXPENSE TRACKER			
ITEM/PURCHASE	STATUS ✓	DATE PAID	TOTAL COST

NOTES & REMINDERS

TOTAL COST:

Notes:

CATERING PLANNER DETAILS

Entertainment Planner

ENTERTAINMENT EXPENSE TRACKER			
ITEM/PURCHASE	STATUS ✓	DATE PAID	TOTAL COST

NOTES & REMINDERS	
	TOTAL COST:

Notes:

Love

ENTERTAINMENT DETAILS

Videographer Planner

VIDEOGRAPHER EXPENSE TRACKER			
ITEM/PURCHASE	STATUS ✓	DATE PAID	TOTAL COST

NOTES & REMINDERS

TOTAL COST:

Notes:

VIDEOGRAPHER DETAILS

Photographer Planner

PHOTOGRAPHER EXPENSE TRACKER			
ITEM/PURCHASE	STATUS ✓	DATE PAID	TOTAL COST

NOTES & REMINDERS	
	TOTAL COST:

Notes:

PHOTOGRAPHER DETAILS

Florist Planner

FLORIST EXPENSE TRACKER

ITEM/PURCHASE	STATUS ✓	DATE PAID	TOTAL COST

NOTES & REMINDERS	
	TOTAL COST:

Notes:

FLORIST PLANNING DETAILS

Extra Wedding Costs

MISC WEDDING EXPENSE TRACKER			
ITEM/PURCHASE	STATUS ✓	DATE PAID	TOTAL COST

NOTES & REMINDERS	
	TOTAL COST:

Notes:

MISC WEDDING DETAILS

Bachelorette Party Planner

EVENT DETAILS

DATE

TIME

VENUE

THEME

HOST

OTHER

GUEST LIST

FIRST NAME	LAST NAME	R

TIME	SCHEDULE OF EVENTS

SUPPLIES & SHOPPING LIST

- [ ]
- [ ]
- [ ]
- [ ]
- [ ]
- [ ]
- [ ]
- [ ]
- [ ]
- [ ]
- [ ]
- [ ]
- [ ]
- [ ]
- [ ]
- [ ]
- [ ]

NOTES & REMINDERS

love

Bachelor Party Planner

EVENT DETAILS

DATE

TIME

VENUE

THEME

HOST

OTHER

GUEST LIST

FIRST NAME	LAST NAME	R

SCHEDULE OF EVENTS

TIME

SUPPLIES & SHOPPING LIST

- [ ]
- [ ]
- [ ]
- [ ]
- [ ]
- [ ]
- [ ]
- [ ]
- [ ]
- [ ]
- [ ]
- [ ]
- [ ]
- [ ]
- [ ]
- [ ]
- [ ]

NOTES & REMINDERS

love

Reception Planner

MEAL PLANNER IDEAS

HORS D'OEUVRES

1st COURSE:

3rd COURSE:

2nd COURSE:

4th COURSE:

MEAL PLANNING NOTES

Wedding Planning Notes

IDEAS & REMINDERS

Wedding to do List

Wedding Guest List

NAME	ADDRESS	PHONE #	# IN PARTY	RSVP: ✓

Wedding Guest List

NAME	ADDRESS	PHONE #	# IN PARTY	RSVP: ✓

Wedding Guest List

NAME	ADDRESS	PHONE #	# IN PARTY	RSVP: ✓

Wedding Guest List

NAME	ADDRESS	PHONE #	# IN PARTY	RSVP: ✓

Wedding Guest List

NAME	ADDRESS	PHONE #	# IN PARTY	RSVP: ✓

Wedding Guest List

NAME	ADDRESS	PHONE #	# IN PARTY	RSVP: ✓

Wedding Guest List

NAME	ADDRESS	PHONE #	# IN PARTY	RSVP: ✓

Wedding Guest List

NAME	ADDRESS	PHONE #	# IN PARTY	RSVP: ✓

Wedding Guest List

NAME	ADDRESS	PHONE #	# IN PARTY	RSVP: ✓

Wedding Guest List

NAME	ADDRESS	PHONE #	# IN PARTY	RSVP: ✓

Wedding Seating Chart

Table

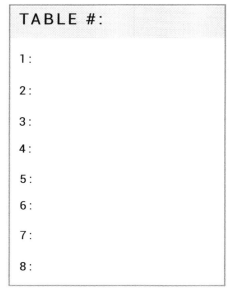

love

Table

Wedding Seating Chart

Table

TABLE #:
1 :
2 :
3 :
4 :
5 :
6 :
7 :
8 :

love

Table

TABLE #:
1 :
2 :
3 :
4 :
5 :
6 :
7 :
8 :

Wedding Seating Chart

Table #

Table #

TABLE #:
1 :
2 :
3 :
4 :
5 :
6 :
7 :
8 :

TABLE #:
1 :
2 :
3 :
4 :
5 :
6 :
7 :
8 :

Wedding Seating Chart

Table #

Table #

TABLE #:
1 :
2 :
3 :
4 :
5 :
6 :
7 :
8 :

TABLE #:
1 :
2 :
3 :
4 :
5 :
6 :
7 :
8 :

Wedding Seating Chart

Table #

Table #

TABLE #:
1 :
2 :
3 :
4 :
5 :
6 :
7 :
8 :

TABLE #:
1 :
2 :
3 :
4 :
5 :
6 :
7 :
8 :

Wedding Seating Chart

Table #

Table #

TABLE #:
1 :
2 :
3 :
4 :
5 :
6 :
7 :
8 :

TABLE #:
1 :
2 :
3 :
4 :
5 :
6 :
7 :
8 :

Wedding Seating Chart

Table #

Table #

TABLE #:
1 :
2 :
3 :
4 :
5 :
6 :
7 :
8 :

TABLE #:
1 :
2 :
3 :
4 :
5 :
6 :
7 :
8 :

Wedding Seating Chart

Table #

TABLE #:
1 :
2 :
3 :
4 :
5 :
6 :
7 :
8 :

Table #

TABLE #:
1 :
2 :
3 :
4 :
5 :
6 :
7 :
8 :

Wedding Seating Chart

Table #

Table #

TABLE #:
1 :
2 :
3 :
4 :
5 :
6 :
7 :
8 :

TABLE #:
1 :
2 :
3 :
4 :
5 :
6 :
7 :
8 :

Wedding Seating Chart

Table #

TABLE #:
1 :
2 :
3 :
4 :
5 :
6 :
7 :
8 :

Table #

TABLE #:
1 :
2 :
3 :
4 :
5 :
6 :
7 :
8 :

Wedding Seating Chart

Table #

Table #

TABLE #:
1 :
2 :
3 :
4 :
5 :
6 :
7 :
8 :

TABLE #:
1 :
2 :
3 :
4 :
5 :
6 :
7 :
8 :

Wedding Seating Chart

Table #

Table #

TABLE #:
1 :
2 :
3 :
4 :
5 :
6 :
7 :
8 :

TABLE #:
1 :
2 :
3 :
4 :
5 :
6 :
7 :
8 :

Wedding Seating Chart

Table #

Table #

TABLE #:
1:
2:
3:
4:
5:
6:
7:
8:

TABLE #:
1:
2:
3:
4:
5:
6:
7:
8:

Wedding Seating Chart

Table #

TABLE #:
1:
2:
3:
4:
5:
6:
7:
8:

Table #

TABLE #:
1:
2:
3:
4:
5:
6:
7:
8:

Wedding Seating Chart

Table #

Table #

TABLE #:
1 :
2 :
3 :
4 :
5 :
6 :
7 :
8 :

TABLE #:
1 :
2 :
3 :
4 :
5 :
6 :
7 :
8 :

Wedding Seating Chart

Table #

Table #

TABLE #:

1:

2:

3:

4:

5:

6:

7:

8:

TABLE #:

1:

2:

3:

4:

5:

6:

7:

8:

Wedding Seating Chart

Table #

TABLE #:
1 :
2 :
3 :
4 :
5 :
6 :
7 :
8 :

Table #

TABLE #:
1 :
2 :
3 :
4 :
5 :
6 :
7 :
8 :

Wedding Seating Chart

Table #

TABLE #:
1 :
2 :
3 :
4 :
5 :
6 :
7 :
8 :

Table #

TABLE #:
1 :
2 :
3 :
4 :
5 :
6 :
7 :
8 :

Wedding Seating Chart

Table #

TABLE #:
1 :
2 :
3 :
4 :
5 :
6 :
7 :
8 :

Table #

TABLE #:
1 :
2 :
3 :
4 :
5 :
6 :
7 :
8 :

Wedding Seating Chart

Table #

TABLE #:
1 :
2 :
3 :
4 :
5 :
6 :
7 :
8 :

Table #

TABLE #:
1 :
2 :
3 :
4 :
5 :
6 :
7 :
8 :

Wedding Seating Chart

Table #

Table #

TABLE #:
1 :
2 :
3 :
4 :
5 :
6 :
7 :
8 :

TABLE #:
1 :
2 :
3 :
4 :
5 :
6 :
7 :
8 :

Wedding Seating Chart

Table #

Table #

TABLE #:
1 :
2 :
3 :
4 :
5 :
6 :
7 :
8 :

TABLE #:
1 :
2 :
3 :
4 :
5 :
6 :
7 :
8 :

Wedding Seating Chart

Table #

Table #

TABLE #:

1:

2:

3:

4:

5:

6:

7:

8:

TABLE #:

1:

2:

3:

4:

5:

6:

7:

8:

Wedding Seating Chart

Table #

TABLE #:

1 :

2 :

3 :

4 :

5 :

6 :

7 :

8 :

Table #

TABLE #:

1 :

2 :

3 :

4 :

5 :

6 :

7 :

8 :

Wedding Seating Chart

Table #

Table #

TABLE #:
1:
2:
3:
4:
5:
6:
7:
8:

TABLE #:
1:
2:
3:
4:
5:
6:
7:
8:

Wedding Seating Chart

Table #

Table #

TABLE #:
1 :
2 :
3 :
4 :
5 :
6 :
7 :
8 :

TABLE #:
1 :
2 :
3 :
4 :
5 :
6 :
7 :
8 :

Wedding Seating Chart

Table

TABLE #:

1:	2:	3:	4:	5:	6:	7:	8:
9:	10:	11:	12:	13:	14:	15:	16:

Table

TABLE #:

1:	2:	3:	4:	5:	6:	7:	8:
9:	10:	11:	12:	13:	14:	15:	16:

Wedding Seating Chart

Table

TABLE #:

1:	2:	3:	4:	5:	6:	7:	8:
9:	10:	11:	12:	13:	14:	15:	16:

Table

TABLE #:

1:	2:	3:	4:	5:	6:	7:	8:
9:	10:	11:	12:	13:	14:	15:	16:

Wedding Seating Chart

Table

TABLE #:

1:	2:	3:	4:	5:	6:	7:	8:
9:	10:	11:	12:	13:	14:	15:	16:

Table

TABLE #:

1:	2:	3:	4:	5:	6:	7:	8:
9:	10:	11:	12:	13:	14:	15:	16:

Wedding Seating Chart

Table #

TABLE #:

1:	2:	3:	4:	5:	6:	7:	8:
9:	10:	11:	12:	13:	14:	15:	16:

Table #

TABLE #:

1:	2:	3:	4:	5:	6:	7:	8:
9:	10:	11:	12:	13:	14:	15:	16:

Wedding Seating Chart

Table

TABLE #:

1:	2:	3:	4:	5:	6:	7:	8:
9:	10:	11:	12:	13:	14:	15:	16:

Table

TABLE #:

1:	2:	3:	4:	5:	6:	7:	8:
9:	10:	11:	12:	13:	14:	15:	16:

Wedding Seating Chart

Table #

TABLE #:

1:	2:	3:	4:	5:	6:	7:	8:
9:	10:	11:	12:	13:	14:	15:	16:

Table #

TABLE #:

1:	2:	3:	4:	5:	6:	7:	8:
9:	10:	11:	12:	13:	14:	15:	16:

Wedding Seating Chart

Table

Table #:

1:	2:	3:	4:	5:	6:	7:	8:
9:	10:	11:	12:	13:	14:	15:	16:

Table

Table #:

1:	2:	3:	4:	5:	6:	7:	8:
9:	10:	11:	12:	13:	14:	15:	16:

Wedding Seating Chart

Table

TABLE #:

1:	2:	3:	4:	5:	6:	7:	8:
9:	10:	11:	12:	13:	14:	15:	16:

Table

TABLE #:

1:	2:	3:	4:	5:	6:	7:	8:
9:	10:	11:	12:	13:	14:	15:	16:

Wedding Seating Chart

Table

TABLE #:

1:	2:	3:	4:	5:	6:	7:	8:
9:	10:	11:	12:	13:	14:	15:	16:

Table

TABLE #:

1:	2:	3:	4:	5:	6:	7:	8:
9:	10:	11:	12:	13:	14:	15:	16:

Wedding Seating Chart

Table

TABLE #:

1:	2:	3:	4:	5:	6:	7:	8:
9:	10:	11:	12:	13:	14:	15:	16:

Table

TABLE #:

1:	2:	3:	4:	5:	6:	7:	8:
9:	10:	11:	12:	13:	14:	15:	16:

Wedding Seating Chart

Table

TABLE #:

1:	2:	3:	4:	5:	6:	7:	8:
9:	10:	11:	12:	13:	14:	15:	16:

Table

TABLE #:

1:	2:	3:	4:	5:	6:	7:	8:
9:	10:	11:	12:	13:	14:	15:	16:

Wedding Planning Notes

IDEAS & REMINDERS

Wedding to do List

PLANNING FOR THE BIG DAY

Wedding Planning Notes

IDEAS & REMINDERS

Wedding to do List

PLANNING FOR THE BIG DAY

Wedding Planning Notes

IDEAS & REMINDERS

Wedding to do List

PLANNING FOR THE BIG DAY

Wedding Planning Notes

IDEAS & REMINDERS

Wedding to do List

Wedding Planning Notes

IDEAS & REMINDERS

Wedding to do List

PLANNING FOR THE BIG DAY

Made in the USA
Las Vegas, NV
26 October 2021